CAPE COD
IN COLOR

CAPE COD
in Color

A Collection of Color

Photographs by

JULIUS LAZARUS

With Text and

Notes on the Illustrations by

MARION VUILLEUMIER

HASTINGS HOUSE · PUBLISHERS

New York, 10016

PUBLISHED 1977 BY HASTINGS HOUSE, PUBLISHERS, INC.

Library of Congress Cataloging in Publication Data
Lazarus, Julius.
    Cape Cod in color.

    (Profiles of America)
    1. Cape Cod—History.   2. Cape Cod—Description and travel.
I. Vuilleumier, Marion.   II. Title.
F72.C3L36   1977   974.4'92   77-11037
ISBN 0-8038-1224-8

Published simultaneously in Canada by
Saunders, of Toronto, Ltd., Don Mills, Ontario

Printed and bound in Hong Kong by Mandarin Publishers Limited

*Appreciation is expressed
to the many people
who provided information
and to Miss Marian Logan
for typing the manuscript.*

CONTENTS

Where Massachusetts Stands
on Her Guard

I

IN NOVEMBER of 1620 a tiny cockleshell called the "Mayflower" rounded the tip of Cape Cod, anchoring in its natural harbor after a perilous trip from England across the vast Atlantic Ocean. According to Pilgrim William Bradford, who was aboard, "being thus safely arrived in a good harbor and brought to safe land, they (the Pilgrims) fell upon their knees and blessed the God of Heaven."

Ever since, judging by the hordes of visitors who flock to the Cape with the regularity of the swallows returning to Capistrano, people have found here good harbors and safe lands. In fact, many have decided to emulate a few of the Pilgrims who left their first tiny village, Plimoth Plantation, to settle on Cape Cod. In recent years this beautiful peninsula has received such an influx of new residents and so many continuous waves of tourists that present day inhabitants fear it will be engulfed. They worry about the effect on the fragile environment.

It is amusing to note that tourists who come to these shores with regularity are apt to encourage others to visit this vacation heaven. "It's the greatest place," they enthuse, "and such a short drive from the eastern cities."

Then as soon as they have purchased Cape Cod property of their very own, they look with critical eyes at the cars streaming across the two automobile bridges that span the Cape Cod Canal. "Why do they keep coming?" grumble these new residents with their sudden proprietory airs. "They use our precious water and clutter up the roads."

But visitors continue to come and no doubt always will, drawn by this carefree playground with its rich historical heritage and its sparkling natural beauty—and of course these visitors are essential to the Cape Cod economy.

Many potential vacation spots long for a flow of visitors such as Cape Cod enjoys without hardly lifting a finger. (I suppose the Chamber of Commerce would not agree wholeheartedly since it does expend considerable energy in that direction.) But seriously, what is the pull of this Lorelei that draws people to its shores as a magnet attracts metal?

Many notable visitors have expressed opinions on this subject. One of the earliest was the Concord sage Henry David Thoreau who made four visits in different years, intrigued by the Cape's unique character.

"Cape Cod is the bared and bended arm of Massachusetts:" wrote he in his book entitled *Cape Cod,* "the shoulder is at Buzzards Bay; the elbow, or crazy bone, at Cape Mallebarre; the wrist at Truro; and the sandy fist at Provincetown—behind which the State stands on her guard, with her back to the Green Mountains, and her feet planted on the floor of the ocean, like an athlete protecting her Bay." Who wouldn't want to see a land described like that?

Henry Beston, author of *The Outermost House,* who spent a year on the Great Beach in a tiny hut that is now a national literary landmark, wrote in the introduction to a later edition of Thoreau's book, "A first glimpse of the great outer beach of Cape Cod is one of the most memorable experiences in all America. As one looks from the height of the earth-cliff which there confronts and halts the North Atlantic, it is the immense and empty plain of ocean which first seizes the imagination, the ocean seen as one of the splendors of earth, and ever reflecting the mood of the season and the day. One may gaze at a mirror of summer blue ending at an horizon taut as a gleaming line; one may stare down into a vast and leaden turbulence of storm roaring ashore under another violence of the sky..."

Suburbanites and city dwellers come here to stand in awe, watching nature unleash her power.

Timothy Dwight, President of Yale University, traveled indefatigably throughout the East in the late 1700's chronicling what he saw for "curious people a hundred years into the future." As his stagecoach lumbered down the rutted Cape roads, he was captivated with the architecture and was the first to use the term Cape Cod house for the homes of less wealthy inhabitants.

Today the fame of the Cape Cod house, usually described as a small, comfortable home with a pitched roof, has spread the world over and pilgrims come to see the originals.

Gladys Taber who writes today at Still Cove, her home overlooking Mill Pond in Orleans, says in *My Own Cape Cod* that this is a very personal place where one can find whatever one seeks but that its charm is particularly its people. "What is Cape Cod? It is a narrow stretch of land jutting into the fathomless sea and so far man has not been able to devastate it so it is beautiful as young love's fragile dreaming. But it is, in actuality, the people who sweep the pine pollen from their doorsteps in season, carry a pot of home-baked beans to a neighbor, knock themselves out to find a home for lost kittens, feed crippled seagulls, fight fiercely at town meetings."

Who wouldn't move hundreds of miles to live among such folks?

Add to this the invigoration and health that fills tired and worried bodies with zest and energy and one can readily see why thousands travel to Cape Cod at the drop of a credit card.

II

ALTHOUGH IT may be hard to believe, there weren't always tourists here. In 1620, there were 30,000 Wampanoags living on this wooded peninsula, in the adjoining forests, and on two offshore islands. Some 30 tribes of native people were banded together under the leadership of a council of chiefs and their Supreme Sachem Massasoit.

This pleasing land, bordered by fine-grained sand and restless blue-green water also abounded with creatures with fins, wings, and four legs. The Wampanoags, who were the original conservationists, knew how to live among these lesser creatures, using them for food but not wasting their offerings. These natives also lived on the land gently, leaving no permanent scars on its face. Only well-traveled foot trails, piles of shells uncovered by shifting sand, and the blackened remains of camp fires were reminders of their passage. Even the permanent Wampanoag lodges, constructed of saplings, bark, seaweed insulation, and vine ties, melted back into the land when no longer needed.

Ancestors of these Wampanoags had seen a succession of would-be tourists and settlers in preceding centuries. The first recorded were Vikings, who about AD 1000 nudged their sharp-prowed ships close to the shores as they searched (unsuccessfully as it turned out) for places to colonize. Later there came waves of explorers sent out by the kings of Europe to bring back anything that could be turned into riches and enhance their reigns. Thick furs and fragrant sassafras filled the returning ships.

Bartholomew Gosnold anchored off the Cape's tip in 1602 and was surrounded by schools of codfish. The explorer caught such a profusion that he immediately named the projection Cape Cod. Though there were later attempts to label the land something else, Gosnold's term stuck. Today a handsome carved "sacred cod" graces the Massachusetts State House in Boston, an ever present reminder that this fish is intimately entangled not only in its fishing lines, but also in the history of the State.

One or two less principled of these early ship captains abducted some of the Wampanoags who had innocently come aboard to trade, planning to exhibit them back home. This act immediately aroused the ire of the natives, prejudicing them against later explorers. Unwittingly this act provided an interpreter for the Pilgrims.

Squanto, a Patucxet of Accomack (the present Plymouth area), was kidnapped by the infamous Captain Thomas Hunt in 1614. He was carried off to Spain but later made his way to England where he was befriended by the merchant John Slanie with whom he lived in London for two years. Making his way finally to Newfoundland, Squanto signed on as a guide to Thomas Dermer, who was exploring along the shore for Sir Ferdinand Georges. Reaching his homeland in 1618, Squanto made the appalling discovery that he was the sole survivor of his tribe which had been wiped out by an epidemic in 1617. Conversant in English and the ways of the white men he was probably one of the first people notified when swift runners brought the news to Supreme Sachem Massasoit of the great canoe that had anchored off the tip of their land.

By this time, Massasoit presided over a council of hawks and doves. Some chiefs were fearful of white men, calling them devils. Others agreed they were not gods, but welcomed their coming because they traded metal knives, axes, and beads. Up until this time the council's hot debates had not needed a final decision. Now, however, the unceasing flow of messages coming from the dark-skinned scouts made it clear these newcomers were here to stay. After preliminary expeditions on the outer Cape, the palefaces had sailed across the Bay and landed in Patucxet territory. Felling trees and building queer looking shelters, they had left their great canoe. Their party, including women and children, now lived in a new settlement on the sloping shore. What were the Wampanoags to do?

Though we don't have a record of the Wampanoag council meetings, we do know that Massasoit and the doves won, thereby unknowingly allowing for a long line of Mayflower descendants as well as mixed emotions on the part of descendants of the Wampanoags. One Wampanoag jocularly told the Massachusetts legislature on the occasion of the Centennial of the incorporation of the Town of Mashpee that Massasoit's welcome was the biggest mistake the Wampanoags ever made! `

Nevertheless, it is a fact that in March of 1621 a native walked boldly up the main path of Plimoth Plantation and said to the astonished Pilgrims, "Welcome Englishman." Massasoit's emissary, Samoset, who had learned a few English words from passing seamen, explained that five days hence the great Chief Massasoit was coming to visit them with his retinue. Squanto, who could speak much better English, would be in the company.

Eyewitnesses to that historic meeting report that Massasoit came from his lodge at Sowams (Bristol, Rhode Island) with his brother Quadequina and 60 braves. They were "tall proper men" dressed in deerskins. Massasoit was "a man who possessed the elements of a great and noble mind and a generous heart. He went to the palefaces who landed in his territory as a King meeting the representatives of a great King over the water of whom he had heard."

The Pilgrims received the Supreme Sachem in ceremonies befitting his rank. The great chief was conducted by an honor guard to a partially built house which had been prepared with a green rug and cushions. Immediately Governor John Carver, also with drum, trumpet, and military escort, joined him. After salutations, the leaders kissed each other's hands, then ate and drank together. The friendly visit concluded with a peace treaty which was to last for 50 years.

III

WE THINK the words "population explosion" are current terms, but these were just as threatening to the white and tan people of those early days.

Pilgrim leaders like Edward Winslow, William Brewster, and Bradford (Carver had died in April of 1621) had chosen to settle in a primeval wilderness away from alien influences. With freedom to worship as they chose, they could best accomplish their aim of recreating a loving community similar to first century Christianity. So they settled in with their 400 books and the Mayflower Compact. These Separatists from the Church of England should not be confused with the Puritans who arrived in Boston a decade later and were not as religiously tolerant.

The first few years were uneventful as Pilgrims and Wampanoags gradually established good relations. There were occasional apprehensions caused by some shenanigans of Squanto, who tried to play both sides to his own advantage, and a short-lived settlement of merrymakers at Merry-Mount (Wollaston). But the great Chief Massasoit aided the Pilgrims in a search for the lost lad John Billington, and the Pilgrims ministered to Massasoit when he seemed on his death bed. So the first tenuous bonds of friendship deepened through the years.

The real problem arose when boatloads of settlers arrived in the 1630's from England, driven out by the civil warfare. Large farms were developing and there was no space for newcomers. Cape Cod seemed an attractive alternate since it was included in the Colony's patent. The Pilgrims had noted the extensive salt marshes, so good for cattle fodder, when they established Aptucxet Trading Post in 1627 and when they had journeyed down Cape to buy corn from the Wampanoags.

In 1637 ten men of Saugus, a community north of Boston began the Town of Sandwich. Two years later the Great Marshes of Barnstable were colonized by a whole congregation who had earlier emigrated to Scituate. That same year, 1639, there were settlers in Yarmouth. A few Plimoth Plantation residents, some First Comers or Mayflower passengers, feeling continual pressure, relocated on the plains of Eastham in 1644. Eventually there would be fifteen towns spread the length of the Cape from Bourne at the neck to Provincetown at its tip. One was Mashpee, the age-old community of the Wampanoags.

When it became clear that there would be less and less territory available to the natives, Quachatisset and other Wampanoag chiefs of the South Sea (dwellers along the shore of Nantucket Sound) registered their ancient deeds with the Plimouth Colony. In 1638 a tract of 13,500 acres was set aside as the Plantation of Mashpee (or Marshpee as it was then spelled). Gradually many of the Cape Wampanoags moved to Mashpee as their own tribal lands shrank.

The Wampanoag hawk party, which had simmered through the years, rose in concert after the death of Massasoit in 1662 and Wamsutta his older son in 1664. The royalties of the Wampanoags, which consisted of a stole, headband, breastplate, and scarlet cloak, now descended upon Pometecom or Metacomet whom the English called Philip. At the age of twenty-four, Pometecom presided over a council of chiefs who increasingly counseled war before the Wampanoags lost all their lands.

Pometecom confided to an English friend, John Borden, "But little remains of my ancestors' domain. I am resolved not to see the day when I have no country." Somberly he watched his territory further eroded as "firewater" caused havoc among his people and colonists continued to exchange kettles, cloth, beads, and knives for native lands.

In June of 1675 the short and bloody King Philip's War began. Fourteen months later the great chief lay dead near Sowams and his people had been almost exterminated. On Cape Cod, where Wampanoags and English had integrated peacefully, there was no fighting.

The population was still exploding, however, laying the seeds for future problems. Unfortunately the newer comers were not all kindly disposed. The Pilgrim ethic no longer controlled the populace. Furthermore, the long arm of the British government was about to reach across the Atlantic and begin a bruising tax program which would give rise a century later to the American Revolution.

IV

WHAT WAS it like here in this now semi-wooded land when whites and tans were settling in? A traveler in the 1700's would have seen sights both familiar and curious.

At the edge of Shawme Pond in Sandwich, a waterwheel rhythmically slapped the rushing brook as the miller in his faded apron ground the produce brought to him by farmers. The huge stones inexorably crushed the tiny kernels and grains became flour and meal as the farmers rejoiced that they no longer had the long trek to Plymouth like their grandparents and great grandparents.

After Thomas Dexter built this mill in 1654, others were set by streams throughout the Cape. Three of these water mills at Brewster, Sandwich and Yarmouth still ceremoniously creak and grind.

Not every village had a convenient stream so residents looked to wind power for turning their produce from the fruit of the land into the makings of bread and pancakes. Did they perhaps recall tales of picturesque windmills of Holland handed down from the First Comers?

Thomas Paine of Eastham somehow became proficient at constructing these Goliaths with the constantly whirling arms. This millwright traveled incessantly up and down the Cape as town after town found money for these sentinels of the meadows. Eastham, Brewster, Yarmouth, Sandwich and Chatham still have these vestiges of the past.

These curious anachronisms powered by wind and water still draw people but now they come "oh-ing" and "ah-ing" as they watch the stones turning, then purchase stone-ground flour or meal. A few come with eagle eyes looking for new-old sources of energy for the 20th Century.

A more curious mill, built for fulling or "making full" home-woven cloth has completely disappeared, though at least four of these were once scattered across the face of the peninsula.

A marker stands in Marstons Mills near the site of the first fulling mill built over a stream in 1689 by Thomas Marcy. The ladies of the surrounding farms wove their cloth on home looms, then brought it here to the fuller. He would tread, scourge, beat, and rinse the material—cleansing it of grease and soil. The result was a fabric that was felted or shrunk to a firmer, softer weave. It could then be cut into dresses, breeches, vests, and cloaks.

Today's textile detectives who seek the locations of these mills should look for beds of teasels, for every fuller used these lowly relatives of the thistle plant to gently remove any knots or burrs from the bolts of cloth before returning them to the owners.

A less curious sight, but just as entrancing was the architecture of Cape Cod, for the houses of the 1700's resemble those of today, with many originals still remaining. At first view these snug structures covered with weathered gray shingles and capped with a steeply pitched roof may seem just charming and picturesque. Those who inquire will soon learn that these homes have much more to their history. They were built low and placed in protected spots to escape the lashing winds and rains. Usually they were faced south to absorb the warmth of the sun and to tell time. As Doris Doane says in *A Book of Cape Cod Houses,* "When the sun shone directly in the front windows the family knew it was noon-time."

This classic story-and-a-half house also expanded with the family. A small "half house" was built first. These can be recognized today by looking for a house front with two windows at one side of the door. When more room was needed, the house became a "three-quarter Cape," or a "house-and-a half" with two windows on one side of the door and one window on the other side. The "full Cape" or "double house" has a center door with two windows on each side. All sizes of these homes were wrapped around massive chimneys which warmed all the rooms and dictated the size of the tiny pitched stairways to the second floor.

There are some prime examples of these houses along Route 6A in Sandwich, Barnstable, and Yarmouth. If you are traveling behind a pokey car on this ancient highway, be forgiving. The occupants are probably identifying half, three-quarter, and full Capes. If excited gestures are seen through the rear window, perhaps they have found a rare bowed or hip roof, fashioned by some long-ago ship's carpenter turned landlubber.

A style of architecture that came early to Cape Cod was the saltbox, popular all over early New England. Its long sloping roof was a distinct advantage for it conserved heat and allowed snow to slide off easily in the rear. The venerable Dillingham House on Route 6A in Brewster, built in 1659 by Quaker Isaac Dillingham, sports such a glorious sweeping roof.

This allusion to Quakers reminds us that, although the Separatists (or Congregationalists) were the first whites to settle on Cape Cod, Quakers and Baptists arrived soon after. Less than a handful of the church buildings that stood in the 1700's are still with us today. Early congregations met in homes, then built simple meetinghouses which were soon outgrown. Many of those that escaped demolition for more expansive structures were leveled by fire, always a danger to early wooden construction.

So, although new congregations were blanketing the Cape, the white steepled churches we see in the center of today's communities would not have been seen by a traveler then.

One notable exception is that 1717 architectural gem, the meetinghouse of the West Parish Church in West Barnstable. Designed in the early colonial tradition and restored in recent years, it has an entrance and pulpit on the broad side.

Quite fittingly the oldest ecclesiastical building on Cape Cod belongs to the Wampanoags of Mashpee. It was built with the assistance of missionary Richard Bourne in 1684. Erected first on Briant's Neck of hand-hewn lumber sent from England, it was moved to its present location on Route 28 in 1717. The simple white frame square structure, twice restored, is surrounded by an ancient burial ground. A reminder of the reverence and devotion of the Wampanoags through the years, it also would have been one of the familiar sights of 200 years ago.

V

THERE HAS always been activity along the shores of this narrow land, though today there is much more emphasis on pleasure.

In the early days men "farmed" the sea as well as the land. Fishermen loaded their dorys with nets and lines and ventured out in search of cod and mackerel. Their catches fed their families and their neighbors. Any left over were dried (or flaked) upon racks set in the sun for later consumption. These fishermen also reaped clams, oysters, lobsters, and other staples and delicacies from the sea.

Two- and three-masted schooners as well as packet boats could be seen at anchor or sailing off the coast. Thomas Huckins of Barnstable regularly imported spirits and powder from Boston by packet. These packets were depended upon to carry essentials back and forth from one town to another. The packet 'Charming Betty' began a regular run from Sandwich to Boston in 1717. (What was there about that year which keeps turning up as influential in the old records?)

Cape Codders soon became water men, realizing it was much easier to travel by sea than overland. Roads, bridges, and stagecoaches were crude, bone-rattling affairs and the future of transportation was quite clearly by water. Unknowingly, these men were in training for the great Clipper Ship era and for the time when whaling ships would range the seven seas. Henry Crocker Kittredge, respected chronicler of ships and men, wrote later that most Cape men knew their way by sea to China better than to Boston by land.

One of the shore activities of early years that is without parallel today took place on Sandy Neck, that long arm of bizarrely shaped sand dunes that lies off Sandwich and Barnstable. Like the Wampanoags before them, the English settlers prized the oil, meat, blubber, and bone from the whales that drifted ashore or that were captured from the surrounding shallow water. There were many of these leviathans off the Cape especially during fall and winter.

Richard Mather, an early traveler, observed in his journal in 1635 "mighty whales spewing up water in the air like smoke of a chimney and making the sea about them white and hoary . . . of such incredible bigness that I will never wonder that the body of Jonah could be in the belly of a whale."

It was not unusual for 200 men to be occupied in off-shore whaling, many waiting in "ye whale house" for these creatures to appear. When watchers in lookout stations saw a whale spouting or spotted the rounded backs of blackfish (a species of small whale), they electrified the crowd with the cry "Whale in the Bay." Men tumbled out of the bunk-houses, jumped into whale boats, and surrounded their quarry. Yelling fiercely and splashing the water with the flat of their oars, they drove the whales toward shore. When beached, the whales were killed and drawn up on the sand with heavy tackle and capstans. The blubber was melted down in one of four tryworks located along the shore and the bones were scraped clean.

Years of these fierce attacks must have frightened off the creatures because by the early 1800's fewer whales were appearing. If the Cape Codders wanted whales, it was clear they would have to outfit ships for long voyages, design portable tryworks, and go after the whales.

By the energetic efforts of the most well-to-do citizens, who sold shares in the voyage, money was accumulated to send ships to the oceans of the world. Many whaling voyages lasted three and four years and launched an era of wild adventure. Dr. John Osborne of Sandwich captured its flavor with the following verse:

"Bold, hardy men, with blooming age,
    Our sandy shores produce
With monstrous fish they dare engage
    And dangerous callings choose."

One of the by-products of these voyages was the art of scrimshaw. Whalemen whiled away the monotony of the days between whale sightings by intricately carving objects of whalebone. Since whales are now endangered species and no new bone will be available, genuine scrimshaw is much sought after by collectors today. The Falmouth Historical Society has a particularly fine collection.

Another shore activity which has disappeared with the passage of the years is salt making. Early fishermen needed salt to preserve their catches of fish. With the on-again, off-again British blockades, salt was often not available. It was also very expensive to import. Ingenious residents, with salt water in their front yards, invented, then refined a process for removing the salt which though slow, was satisfactory and cheap.

Water was drawn up from the ocean by windmills and chanelled into a series of tight water vats. Movable roofs were attached which could shelter the vats in rain and be moved off in sunshine. Visitors curious about this long-ago process can examine a working model at the Aptucxet Trading Post in Bourne and can even go away clutching a vial of the product.

In the early 1800's saltworks ringed the shores and became a major industry in all the towns. At its peak around 1830 there were 442 windmills busily whirling up water which dried into half a million barrels of salt. As new salt mines were discovered elsewhere and salt could be imported more cheaply, the windmills ceased turning and the vats were recycled into other building. Carpenters, whose tools later became rusty working with the briny old boards, viewed salt making as a mixed blessing.

VI

LIKE OTHER adolescents the world over, Cape Cod had its growing pains. The struggle for maturity came not only as its inhabitants turned their energies to more elaborate buildings or into unique industries, but also as the clamor of human problems reached them from the outside world. Every few decades, it seems, these clashes erupted into wars which affected Cape Codders and their ways of living.

Scarcely was the King Philip's War over, when a call came for Cape men to ferry British troops ashore in Canada during the French and Indian Wars. The shallow-draft whale-boats were ideal for this purpose and experienced whalemen were needed. Gorham's of Barnstable, first John and then sons Shubel and David, headed expeditions intermittently from 1690 to 1763, when peace was finally declared.

It must have seemed a scant respite to the weary residents who were busy raising money to pay for these forays before the shots at Lexington and Concord signaled the start of the American Revolution. To be sure, Cape Codders were aware new trouble was brewing, for two of their own were partly responsible for ringing up the curtain on this uprising against the King and Parliament of England.

James Otis, Jr., fiery Boston lawyer and political activist, and his sister Mercy Otis Warren, Plymouth author and satirist, were born on the Great Marshes of West Barnstable—and their careers were followed with interest and sympathy back home. Cape Committees of Correspondence were already in touch with the Boston-based Sons of Liberty, and Liberty Poles stood on many Cape town greens when the call to arms came following that fateful April 19, 1775.

The rigorous previous years of war were as nothing compared to the hardships during the war for independence. Men, bullets, food, and clothing were requisitioned, leaving women and children to work the farms. British ships constantly patrolled offshore, capturing American supplies and keeping Cape Codders in a high state of nerves. By the time the war ended the towns were drained dry. Trade was non-existent and fishing boats doomed to rot by the British blockade were beyond repair. Massachusetts—sometimes referred to today as "Taxachusetts"—has not been known to excuse residents from paying taxes. In 1782, however, a committee from the General Court reported that "said towns are incapable of complying therewith any further," and the State treasurer was instructed to "recall the issues for taxes . . . until further ordered." That shows what a state Cape Cod was in.

Barely had the Cape recovered from the Revolution before the War of 1812 came along to deliver another knockout blow to its sea trade, which was its lifeblood. Not only were vessels officially ordered to stay home by the new nation's embargo, but the British patrols were everywhere, making sure boats were bottled up in the harbors.

The conduct of Commodore Richard Ragget of the British ship 'Spencer' was particularly outrageous. He sailed along the Cape shore threatening to burn the towns unless they came across with ransom payments. Some towns reluctantly dug up the required money, but others refused to be intimidated. Orleans residents, whose counterparts today still cherish Ragget's original letter with its ransom demand, refused to be intimidated.

"I call upon you to come forward with a contribution of one thousand dollars for the preservation of your salt-works which I consider to be a public utility and which otherwise will be destroyed," wrote Ragget, giving October 6th, 1814, as the deadline.

When the British ship arrived that day, every able-bodied man in town, backed by the Barnstable County Militia, fired enough volleys to turn back the redcoats, giving Ragget his answer.

Falmouth residents were just as firm, repulsing the British ship 'Nimrod' that same year. Present day residents like to point to the Nimrod Club building which once stood on the shore and still carries a cannonball fired by the British that fateful day.

Once hostilities were ended between England and America, it was business as usual along the shores of Cape Cod Bay and Nantucket Sound. Commerce blossomed as seamen brought rare silks and china from the Orient and whalers left to chase the leviathans of the deep. At the same time distant travel became normal, this forearm of Massachusetts began to realize it was attached to the rest of the Commonwealth. Because of the railroad, land travel had improved and overland trade began in earnest.

The first train puffed into Sandwich in 1848 to the cheers of fishermen who

22

could ship their catch quicker to eastern cities and to the hoots of packet and stagecoach owners who recognized stiff competition. The majority of residents agreed with Rev. A. J. Church of Wellfleet who wrote:

"The Great Atlantic Railroad for old Cape Cod, all hail!
Bring on the locomotive; lay down the iron rail."

Deming Jarvis, Boston entrepreneur who had chosen Sandwich for the site of his Boston and Sandwich Glass Company in 1825, welcomed the railroad with open arms. Beginning with blown glass, he had progressed to moulded and pressed glass, inventing new procedures which allowed production of glass in quantity. Now his iridescent jewel-like wares could quickly reach the outside world.

Cranberry growers also eagerly awaited the advance of the iron horses down the Cape and rejoiced when they reached Provincetown in 1873. Now ruby fruit from the bogs could be shipped at harvest time to the rest of the country. Cranberries had been around long before the white men arrived, but their bitter taste puckered the mouth. They were better left for the birds (or cranes), which is how these crane-berries got their name. Francis Howard reported in the *Cape Cod Compass*, "About the time white sugar became plentiful some enterprising housewife tried simmering them in sugar—and presto! No crane has been able to get a bill into one since." Something like 45 per cent of the nation's supply comes from the large and small bogs of southeastern Massachusetts—the same bogs that double as skating ponds in the winter when they are flooded to protect the tender vines.

While iron horses were revamping life on land, Cape Cod clipper ships were knifing swiftly through the seas. There had always been boat builders along these shores, but it took the Shivericks of East Dennis to build the big ones. By 1862, Asa and his three sons had launched eight full-rigged ships of which '*Belle of the West*' and '*Wild Hunter*' were probably the most famous. Though this boat yard is long gone, there are many vintage ones like the Crosby's of Osterville still sending seasoned designs like the catboats and Wianno Seniors into the water.

But another storm was brewing that would soon break into Civil War as Abolitionists and adherents of slavery squared off. Cape Codders laid down their oars, furled their sails, and headed off to war. Anti-slavery sentiment was strong here and an underground railroad slipped escaping black folks across the Cape to freedom in Canada as Abolitionist seamen smuggled them in by ship from the South.

The close of the Civil War brought trauma. This was the end of Cape Cod's seafaring era. No longer would the majority of its people earn a living from the sea. A strike had closed the Sandwich Glass factory for good. The bottom had fallen out of the salt market. Whaling was centered elsewhere. The fledgling cranberry industry was growing, but could not support all its people.

Doldrums descended upon the villages. Young men left to earn a living in eastern cities. The population melted from 35,990 before the Civil War to 27,000 by 1900.

Like any young adult worth her salt, Cape Cod faced the troubles squarely. Her people were never known as defeatists. They set out to survey the situation, desperately searching for a new industry. The most promising seemed to be "collecting seaweed to make something for deadening sound in lining walls." But this died aborning for lack of a market.

A few adventurous souls left to seek their fortune in western gold fields, never dreaming there was a pot of gold waiting to be uncovered at home.

VII

AT THE dawn of the 20th Century, Cape Cod literally stood alone. Because of the expertise of capitalist August Belmont, who succeeded where many earlier dreamers had failed, the Cape Cod Canal made this peninsula an island. The surgery, which took five years, was completed in 1914 and was greeted with rejoicing. Now the tug-pulled barges, which had supplanted the earlier packet boats, could carry their enormous loads safely along the coast without facing the hazardous reefs lurking in the outer Cape waters. Fourteen years later this monumental private enterprise was purchased by the government and became one of our nation's commercial lifelines.

Three bridges, two for cars and one for the railroad, linked Cape Cod to the mainland. Travelers riding across the spans or driving beside the waterway often incredulously sight ocean-going vessels of tremendous size passing serenely by. There are those who still remember driving in the evening to the canal's edge to watch the New York boat pass through. The dance orchestra could clearly be heard and there was much waving between passengers and onlookers.

The eight-mile-long stretch was a perfect place for the breathtaking 1976 Bicentennial Parade of Tall Ships. What a sight it was to see the '*Regina Maris*', full sails set, emerge from the mists at the canal's southern entrance and majestically sail between the crowd-lined banks to the salute of muskets, the whistle of tugs, and the watery plumes of escorting fireboats.

A traveler in this century sees changes beyond the canal. A drive to Provincetown reveals larger and grander houses, shopping centers and stores, but most of all crowds of people everywhere.

Church steeples and towers point skyward in profusion. Some are topped

24

with crosses, for Roman Catholics and Episcopalians have spread along the peninsula along with many other religious recent comers. Eventually these grew to 136 congregations representing 30 denominations. Some, like the Baha'i, have no building. A few congregations worship in homes. A few chapels are only open in summer. Some consider themselves religious societies rather than churches, but all have considerable impact on Cape Cod life.

Along with religious faiths came the people who brought them—a veritable patchwork of skin color and nationality. Signs over shops and eating places, names in the telephone book testify to the variety of people who now call Cape Cod home. The Portuguese of Provincetown and East Falmouth and the Finns of West Barnstable still have fairly well-defined enclaves. Others like the Greeks, Irish, and Jews are less centralized, settling in among their neighbors as have the Blacks.

These folks have added an unmistakable flavor to Cape Cod life. It's possible to drop into a bakery for Finnish nisu (sweet bread) and Limppu (black bread), then step down the street to another store for Linguisa (Portuguese sausage) as well as their sweet bread. Those in the know can direct shoppers to a Greek store where they can secure Baklava, that Near East confection of wafer-thin pastry drenched with honey and nuts.

While the population was flourishing in ways the First Comers never imagined in their wildest dreams, the hidden pot of gold was gradually coming to light. Visitors had been drawn here as far back as Indian days when Wampanoags left their permanent lodges inland to spend the summer at the shore. During the Colony period Dutch traders, soldiers on missions, and officials traveling on government business needed places to stay. So the enterprising citizens added ells to their ordinaries, as inns were then called.

Anthony Thacher was the first "keeper of the ordinary" in Yarmouth, being authorized to draw wine in 1644. During stagecoach days these oases for thirsty and tired travelers stretched in a chain along the Cape. Picture signs, required by law since many people could not read, had such exhortations as:

"Pull up your ropes and anchor here
Till better weather doth appear."
or
"Pause, Traveler here, just stop and think
a weary man must need a drink."

One of these original inns, Fessenden's at Sandwich, tenaciously lasting through several changes of ownership and a major fire, has metamorphosed today into the authentically decorated Daniel Webster Inn.

From these rather tenuous beginnings has grown the resort industry, Cape

Cod's economic mainstay. Though its growth was not clearly seen in the last century, some residents could see glimmers on the horizon.

As early as 1870 a few forward-looking businessmen chartered the Hyannis Land Company, buying up a thousand acres along the south shore. They laid out Hyannis Port, and people flocked in by private railroad car and steam yacht to spend the summer in this "first-class watering place." The little village was a summer playground of governors, generals, attorney-generals, and cabinet members long before Joseph P. Kennedy bought a home at the end of Marchant Avenue and laid the cornerstone for the world-famous Kennedy Compound.

Falmouth, Chatham, Provincetown, and all the communities in between were soon catering to those with average pocketbooks as well as the well-to-do. With the coming of the motor car and the unwinding of miles of macadam ribbon, middle class folks could afford to come for the weekend or for their vacations. Day-trippers relaxed on the soft sands and bathed in the warm water. Spare rooms were rented, tiny overnight cottages erected, and gradually more and more motels built. Roadside stands offered beach plum jelly. It was full steam ahead for the resort business. The pot of gold at the end of the rainbow was in sight.

Cape Codders were delighted to find the growing resorts engendered many spin-off businesses. Vacationers wanted to play golf, buy sailfishes, own yachts, charter fishing boats, and shop for souvenirs. Automobiles swallowed gasoline and vacationers wanted to eat out. Garages and restaurants flourished. Waitresses rushing to work and jean-clad workers driving up to man the gas pumps became a familiar though seasonal sight.

Two cataclysmic world wars upset the resort trade only temporarily. With a demand for workers at nearby shipyards and at the burgeoning Otis Air Force Base, the economy whirled along in high gear. Residents of the fifteen towns enlisted in the armed forces and used their skills in the Merchant Marine.

When peace came, Cape Codders, heaving long sighs of relief, began again to capitalize on their natural treasures. They were agreeably surprised to find a boom in retirement dwellings. Many 65-year-olds were moving here permanently, drawn by the comparatively mild climate and the substantially smaller winter snows. These white heads energetically played golf almost the year round. It was soon obvious that a hearty welcome to more of these folks would pump new money into the Cape coffers year round. Building and related trades perked up. Organizations for retired people sprang up like dandelions in spring grass. Many of these retirees signed up for countless hours of volunteer activity, making life richer for all ages.

Some of their services were given to the arts. One vigorous retiree, who volunteers at the Cape Cod Conservatory of Music and Art, wrote, "When my wife and I decided to retire to Cape Cod four years ago, some of our friends suggested we were moving to a cultural desert." His off-Cape friends didn't realize one can literally trip over many other art groups like the Cape Cod Art Association, craftsmen's guilds, and musical organizations of all types. Would you believe the Town of Barnstable alone has over 100 groups to enrich life and give human services?

Artists are here too. A *New York Times* atricle recently noted, "The Cape is the working, producing side of the East Coast art scene." When Charles Hawthorne opened the Cape Cod School of Art in Provincetown in 1899, would he have imagined that seven decades later 60 major artists would be producing their works on this sandy projection?

Writers have also found this a haven. Over 150 authors live or summer here if one goes by the guest lists compiled annually by the Cape Cod Writers' Conference. People of letters are gratified to find a place so secluded yet so convenient to agents and publishers in New York and Boston.

Exciting theater is part of the scene on this narrow land. The Provincetown players began first in 1915. A year later they were joined by staunch supporter, playwright Eugene O'Neill. Three times winner of Pulitzer prizes and once a Nobel winner, he focused world attention on the little theater-on-the-wharf.

The continuing surge of summer vacationers provided enthusiastic audiences for summer stock beginning with the Cape Playhouse in Dennis in 1927. The very first production, "The Guardsman" with Basil Rathbone, launched its still deserved reputation as the "cradle of the stars." Community theaters currently present top plays year round augmented by college productions and professional companies in summer.

A land that has generated all this activity in three-quarters of a century and continues to attract more fans is itself quite a star.

VIII

So AT last this well-loved strand has come of age. Though its problems still remain, we love it just the same. Quite obviously we wouldn't exchange it for any other dwelling place.

It's enchanting and compelling as well as annoying and exasperating. It's especially the latter to one who is trying to convey the essence of this very special place in strictly limited pages. No other comparable peninsula has so many attractions per square mile. How painful to ignore so many. This brief sketch can only be considered a starting place for a treasure hunt.

The population explosion that worried the Pilgrims and the Wampanoags is still with us. We now number close to 100,000 people more or less. More when the summer crowds quadruple our numbers and less when retirees escape what winter we have by slipping away to summery climes. The Brewster author and naturalist, John Hay, warns us that "unrestrained growth is our own chief enemy." We wonder. Can we legally limit growth?

The conservationists and the businessmen are still locked into seemingly constant controversy. The Wampanoags, conservationists to the core, have done something about it. Planting their feet firmly on their ancestral lands in Mashpee, they have gone on the "lawpath" and said "Stop" to the advancing bulldozers. Shall the rest of us allow our green trees to be felled by house builders? Can these natural acres be saved for the renewal of humans and animals?

Is there a way to accommodate both?

The men and women in the fifteen towns hear conflicting stories and are faced with vital and sometimes irrevocable decisions. Shall they allow the federal government to permit offshore rigs to suck the energy-producing deposits or should this be prohibited because of the danger to sea life and the unprotected shore? What shall be done about the mounting piles of trash hauled daily to town dumps? Where is that fine line between the marsh land on which building is a "no no" and solid ground where it is allowed?

"The Creator made the world—come and see it" reads an Indian prayer. The Cape Cod National Seashore Park preserves thousands of unique acres—sand dunes, cedar swamps, salt marshes, and scrub forests—but still more needs to be saved if succeeding generations will be able to "come and see it."

As the King of Siam has said so many times on Cape Cod stages during performances of the musical, "The King and I," "It's a puzzlement."

If the past sends us any message, though, it is that the sturdy stock inhabiting this fragile yet eternal place will be equal to the challenge.

THE PLATES

SHAWME POND SWANNERY

Graceful swans swimming majestically in Shawme Pond are the focus of a canvas of New England at its best. The tall spire of the First Church of Christ in Sandwich, piercing resolutely through the foliage, is reminiscent of the many churches which are spiritual anchors set in the center of most villages. Though the parish dates to the town's founding in 1637, this spacious colonial style building was erected in 1847. The steeple is a bit like one in London designed by English architect Sir Christopher Wren. This explains why the term "Wren" church is persistently attached to the building though Wren died long before the church was built.

Around the placid pond are other reminders of earlier times, a grist mill, an ancient cemetery, the 18th Century Greek Revival style town hall, and the restored Deacon Eldred house with its Thornton Burgess exhibits. In the place of honor stands a replica of the town's Liberty Pole around which Tories were forced by Patriots in Revolutionary times to swear allegiance to the new country. Seen sitting squarely on its sturdy foundation across the pond is a house that sheltered families for many winters and that now houses community organizations. Though the people, their needs, and community responses change through the years, it is comforting to have scenes like this remain forever, capturing the essence of times past.

DEXTER GRIST MILL

Fluttering ducks hoping for a handout and flocks of tourists with clicking cameras surround this ancient mill on Shawme Pond in the center of Sandwich almost any day in the year. Built in 1654 by Thomas Dexter, the mill's creaking and groaning mechanism has been a familiar sound through the years as it ground native-grown corn. In the latter part of the 19th Century, when new methods of milling took over, the waterwheel provided power for carding and cloth dressing, marble working, wheelwrighting, tag making, and printing. After that it was a nostalgic backdrop for a tea room and the Old Mill Gift Shop. Restored by the town in 1961, the old mill is grinding once again each summer. Its waterwheel, main drive shaft, and gears ponderously turn the grinding stone. The resulting cornmeal is tucked into many a pocket along with appropriate recipes and eventually results in mouth-watering bread, pancakes, and muffins like those enjoyed by families of long ago.

MAGNIFICENT SANDWICH GLASS

The chimneys that kept a constant pall of smoke over Sandwich for 63 years are long gone. The fiery furnaces that consumed over 2,000 acres of forests have been demolished. The gaffers (glass blowers) no longer use their leather lungs to create exquisite glass pieces at the end of their twirling blowing irons. But the jewel-like products of this industry which employed 500 at its peak still can be seen at the Sandwich Historical Society's Glass Museum.

The demure exterior with its colonial entrance gives no hint of the magnificent treasures inside. Blown, pressed, and lacy glass can be seen in sapphire blue, jade green, golden ruby, amethyst, and salmon pink as well as clear. Some of the finest glassblowers in the world came to Sandwich, including an English expert who taught the technique of making opalescent glass, Nicholas Lutz of Alsace who was famous for paper weights and fine blown glass decorated with glass threads, and Adolphe Bonique of France who wrought creations as fine as any from famed Venice, Italy.

The company's founder, Deming Jarves, loved fine glass but he also determined to produce glass for the average pocketbook, so he developed pressed glass made in steel moulds. Soon tableware and candlesticks poured out of the factory in quantity and were eagerly snapped up by average citizens. Examples of all of these are on display in this outstanding museum. Amid the more formal pieces are a few clever novelties, "off-hand" creations made by glassmen who spent free time making gifts for their wives and sweethearts. Engraving, etching, and cutting add beauty to the infinite variety of objects.

WHERE ELECTRIC POWER DOESN'T MATTER

Overlooking Shawme Pond in Sandwich, the Hoxie House is a superb 17th Century home, considered to be the oldest on Cape Cod still standing on its original location. Though it is rumored a brick labeled 1637 was once found, local sources place the house a bit later. Records state that Rev. John Smith occupied it from 1657 to 1689. In any event the weathered, shingled, two-story building has the thick walls, tiny diamond-paned windows, gunstock corner posts, and chamfered beams of an ancient dwelling. When Smith, his wife, and thirteen children occupied it, his brood must have enjoyed lounging on the wide windowsill seats and scampering up the ladder to the loft beds.

Owned by the Smith family until 1856, the house was purchased by Captain Abraham Hoxie, a whaler who bestowed his name upon it. In 1959 the now classic structure was restored to the 1676-1680 period by the town. Authentic furnishings were loaned by the Museum of Fine Arts in Boston. Dried herbs from the garden, cooking pots by the huge fire-place, and wool lying near the spinning wheel give the impression the occupants just walked out the door.

In several Cape Cod communities ancient homes like this have been rescued and restored so that life as it used to be can be illustrated. It is comforting to know that when blackouts cripple normal town life there are a few places where meals can be cooked, fireplaces can give warmth, candles can give light, and bread can be baked quite independently of electric power.

HISTORIC CANNONS GUARD BARNSTABLE COURTHOUSE

The two cannons on the lawn of the county courthouse in Barnstable village once protected the town from the British during the war of 1812 though they never fired a shot. When swashbuckling Commodore Richard R. Ragget of His Majesty's British ship, the 50-gun '*Spencer*', ranged the bay threatening destruction along with sister ships, the 50-gun '*Newcastle*' and the 54-gun '*Majestic*', Barnstable's worried citizens held a meeting in the Masonic Hall. It was decided to oppose the British and appeal to the Governor for help. Loring Crocker, who had extensive saltworks along the shore, hauled four cannon by ox team from Boston and set them up in strategic locations. Whether it was this menacing sight or the difficulties of getting across the sandy bar no one is sure, but the British turned and sailed away. Joyful celebrants shot the cannon exuberantly for years on the Fourth of July and the number dwindled to two.

The imposing gray granite structure looming behind these two guardians has been the scene of county court since 1832. Like the cannons, it conveys something of a bluff. Those enormous pillars are not completely of stone as one might suppose, but are hollow. There is no bluff about what goes on inside, however, and cases have increased so heavily that this building has spawned both a large addition and an adjacent new court building in spite of the fact that a second district court was added recently in Orleans.

DENNIS CHURCH GUARDS A GRAVEYARD

Author Harriot Barbour in a light piece entitled "The Great Graveyard Controversy" in the anthology, *Cape Cod Sampler*, notes that burial history has four stages. "First came the ingathering of the remains of departed members on family acres. Later the church in its yard sheltered the congregation in death as in life. Then the cemetery became a community of the dead wholly separated from the world of the living; while today brings the happy holiday euphemism of the memorial park." Dennis Union Church represents the second stage. Set back from the hustling Route 6A traffic, it stands guard over the departed night and day, summer and winter.

The typical New England meetinghouse was built by the Evangelical Congregational Society in 1828, one of three groups resulting when the original parish split apart. In 1866 the members welcomed back the other groups (bye gones are apt to be bygones after a generation), and reorganized into the Dennis Union Religious Society. Worshippers were called to services by a schoolhouse hand bell until the Bell Circle, made up of young ladies of the town, raised enough money to buy a bell and clock for the tower. When the parish house was added in 1954, the stage and lighting in Fellowship Hall were given by friends in memory of Actress Gertrude Lawrence. It was just down the street at the Cape Playhouse that the star gave many memorable performances. Quite fittingly part of the playhouse building began life as the Nobscusset Meeting House where ancestors of Dennis Union Church members once worshipped.

42

DENNIS PATRIARCH

One of the pleasures of Cape Cod is moseying along Route 6A and. finding treasures at every turn. (Sometimes peripatetic travelers heard to boast of barreling down the Mid-Cape Highway to Provincetown and "seeing" the Cape in a day cause Cape lovers to shudder.)

Since the gently curving much older road was once the King's Highway and before that the Wampanoag trail to the Cape tip, the gems found along the way span several centuries. One Yarmouth turn, for example, brings enchanted travelers face to face with a 20th Century watering trough framed with a wrought iron arch displaying soaring ducks, a pointing spaniel, and a high-stepping horse. Around the curve is a 19th Century building that began life as a general store but now has books overflowing the front steps and stacked against outside walls.

A town or two later, the fascinating drive brings this 18th Century two-story colonial-style home into view. Typical of many built on the upper Cape, the privately-owned stately patriarch represents a style made popular first in Boston. The early Pilgrim church frowned on ostentation, teaching that a wealthy man should live as simply as his neighbors. But as sea captains brought home great fortunes and the church's influence became less pervasive, these more elaborate homes began to appear in Sandwich and they spread gradually down the Cape.

44

SESUIT BEACH PLAYGROUND

At the entrance of Sesuit Harbor in Dennis is a stretch of sand long a favorite playground. It is busiest in summer when the golden sun shines on the soft sand and when warmer waves ceaselessly roll ashore to challenge the sailor, tug at swimmers, and tease wading toddlers. A chattering family arrives with well-filled picnic basket. Towheaded Huck Finns trudge up the beach with fishing poles and buckets. A gaggle of teenagers cavort in the water like dolphins. Determined sunbathers carefully oil themselves and turn with the precision of a duck on a spit. The crash of waves and the cacophony of voices provide a soothing background.

It is only when the day dims and people leave with their beach towels and umbrellas that tiny creatures warily return. Sandpipers and sanderlings come first, almost as the last person departs. Darting after the receding waves, they snatch tiny shrimps and mollusks from the wet sand then scurry back up the beach before the next wave crashes. Seagulls swoop down looking for shellfish. Finding prizes, they fly high to drop them on a deserted bit of macadam, then descend to pry the tasty morsels from the broken shells. Out of tiny holes in the sand come fiddler crabs, so-called because "the male carries an enormous claw as though it was about to play a violin" explains John F. Waters in *Exploring New England Shores*. "It scurries around . . . looking for bits of plant food. If it feels vibrations from a heavy-footed beachcomber, it disappears." While these wild things play, the wind tugs at the beach grass, etching circles in the sand. As darkness deepens, mice, raccoons, and an occasional deer leave tracks. All too soon it is sunrise and the perpetual playground braces for another onslaught.

THE DILLINGHAM HOUSE OF BREWSTER

Sometime in the mid 1600's, John Dillingham moved from Sandwich to become one of this town's first settlers. His name is perpetuated in this beautiful old saltbox home that stands by tree-shaded Route 6A. Reputed to be the second oldest house on Cape Cod, it dates to about 1659. Tradition says the bricks and some of the other materials used in its construction came from England as ship's ballast. The profile of the house reveals a long sweeping roof which looks like old-fashioned salt containers, hence the name of this style of architecture, which is less common on the Cape than in other parts of New England.

Though the house has remained firm on its foundation, it has been part of three communities. First settlers called their village by its Indian name, Sauquatucket, because they had purchased the land from the heirs of Sachem Napaiotan. In 1694 two John Dillinghams, father and son, joined twenty-two other settlers in a petition to Boston officials for a town of their own and the area became Harwich. When friction arose between the North Parish and the South Parish, the northern part was set off in 1803 as the town of Brewster.

48

ROCK HARBOR, ORLEANS

The serene harbor on the bay side of town is surrounded by quiet marshes and gentle shores that seem an unlikely setting for a battle. Yet it was here during the War of 1812 that townspeople repulsed British troops who were sent to collect tribute. A historic marker notes the site and recounts the story which was reenacted during the Bicentennial in a tremendously moving drama.

Today Rock Harbor is a haven for pleasure and fishing boats but a whiff of the tangy sea air is a reminder of earlier years when many of its citizens were prominent seafarers. Boys began their apprenticeship early, signing aboard as soon as they could climb the rigging—some at the tender age of ten. One of the town's outstanding seamen was Captain Ebeneezer Harding Linnell, world famous captain of the clipper ship Eagle Wing. Charmed by a French villa he saw in Marseilles, the captain commissioned his father-in-law Edmund Crosby to build one just like it. The mansion on Skaket Road which is still a showplace, is a short drive from Rock Harbor.

EASTHAM'S GRIST MILL

Across from Town Hall on Route 6 stands the oldest working wind-driven mill on the Cape. Dominating a sweeping central green it looks much as it did in the long ago when miller Seth Knowles and later John Fulcher set the sails, then would "swing her into the wind's eye, fill the hopper, and give the lift-wheel a spin," says Joseph Berger writing as Jeremiah Digges in *Cape Cod Pilot*. If the miller wasn't feeling his "dispepsy" too much, he would let watching kids "go aloft, up in the cap, and see her great fan-shaft—bigger timber it was, than a Grand Banker's main boom—her great hand-hewn gear and the massive spindle that turned the stone down on the grist deck."

Though the date 1793 is on a board inside, the mill is much older. Tradition says the mill was built in Plymouth about 1688 and then dismantled about one hundred years later and shipped across the Bay. Erected in Truro about 1788 it reached its final Eastham stop in 1793. The long arms turned regularly, cutting great circles in the sky, until around 1900, then lay idle until the town bought it and opened it for public viewing each summer beginning in 1936. Now completely restored, the ancient workings can be closely examined. The seven-foot handmade peg wheel, the homely old stone, and the weathered oak frame are just as able to grind today as when the old miller ground his neighbor's corn for his "pottle" of two quarts to a bushel.

THE PENNIMAN HOUSE'S UNUSUAL GATE

Eastham's famed deep-water whaleman Captain Edward Penniman determined on his retirement to have the fanciest house in town. In 1876 with architectural plans from France the wealthy seaman proceeded to build a French Empire (Victorian) style mansion on Governor Prence Road. The mansard roof and cupola contribute to the impression of opulence which is reinforced by a matching barn. Part of the Cape Cod National Seashore Park property in the Fort Hill area, the house is beautifully kept and a watchful eye is always on the unusual back gate. Once a familiar sight in whaling villages, the whale jawbone gateway is now a rarity since whales are among our endangered species. The process of making bloody jawbones pristine enough to make an attractive frame for picture snapping is a tribute to the ingenuity of Cape Codders who never put excessive energy into a project if there was an easier way to do it. Some alert soul realized that tiny insects who inhabit Cape sands would satisfactorily scour the bones if given the opportunity. So the gory bones were buried for a year, then dug up triumphantly and set in the gateway.

54

WELLFLEET'S WOODEN PIER

There is still one large wooden pier in Wellfleet, that lower Cape town which made its living from the sea and which today looks more like an 1870 seacoast village than any of its neighbors. Fine harbors, prolific oyster beds, passable farming soil, good bay fishing, as well as some of the best spots for offshore whaling attracted settlers. The Indians had been enjoying succulent oyster feasts long before. But it was the deep-water whaling and fishing that brought in the town's money. Its ships were second in number only to Provincetown as over 100 Wellfleet schooners once helped feed the country.

It was in the 1800's at the height of this activity that the famous wharves of Wellfleet began to appear. Harding's Wharf was the first, constructed in 1830. It was soon followed by Commercial, then Enterprise, Central, and finally Mercantile in 1870. Dozens of other unnamed ones joined these in ringing Duck Creek and spilling over along Mayo Beach. Ship chandlers, storekeepers, and salt makers were supporting workers to the seafarers. Today fishermen still mend nets and sally forth to fish though now countless pleasure boats dot the shores. It was from this town that Lorenzo Dow Baker began his sea career at the age of ten and eventually founded the United Fruit Company. Dow also launched the resort business, a present economic mainstay, by building the Chequesset Inn in 1888.

56

UNCLE TIM'S BRIDGE, WELLFLEET

The salt marshes and wetlands that edge the protected shores of Cape Cod necessitate wooden catwalks like Uncle Tim's Bridge to span the tidal creeks. Interested spectators wander across the surrounding tidal marshes examining the marine life. Fiddler crabs scratch in and out of tiny holes. Blackbirds screech at quahoggers. Redwings, sparrows, and meadowlarks nest in its high marsh grass. Mussels, oysters, scallops, horseshoe crabs, and clams abound. The marsh grass turns green in spring and fades into brown tones in colder weather. Once farmers cut salt hay for cattle fodder and bedding. Peat retrieved from the marshes provided welcome heat. Now the marshes are more protected and make a pleasing setting for towns like Wellfleet.

Towering over the town and Bay is the First Congregational Church which was founded in 1723, years before the town itself was set apart from Eastham. Called Billingsgate at first, the town was named Wellfleet when it was incorporated in 1763. This, the congregation's fourth building, was erected in 1850. Designed by carpenter-architects in the classical Greek Revival period, it has a monumental entrance, simple cupola, and belfry, long a landmark to sailors. The tower houses "the only town clock in the world striking ship's bells" according to Ripley's *Believe It or Not*.

CAPE COD LIGHT OVERLOOKS THE GREAT BEACH

On top of what Rev. Levi Whitman once called "a mountain of solid clay in Truro," Cape Cod Light stands sentry duty above the Great Beach which is now part of the Cape Cod National Seashore Park. Ahead is 3,000 miles of Atlantic Ocean. Below the waves crash unceasingly, slowly eating away the blue clay bluff of the Highlands. In calmer weather it is an awe-inspiring sight and surfers would be challenged by waves unlike any on the Cape's more protected shores. In a storm, the mood is fierce and wild. According to Thoreau it is "like being on the deck of a vessel, or rather at the masthead of a man-of-war thirty miles at sea."

Cape Cod Light (or Highland Light) was the Cape's first lighthouse, with its initial version built in 1797. Isaac Small, the first keeper, was kept busy filling, trimming, and lighting twenty-four whale oil lamps. In addition he worked an "eclipser" which made the light a flashing beacon so seamen wouldn't confuse it with the Boston light. Rebuilt in 1857 and electrified in 1932, the lighthouse now uses a 1,000-watt bulb which is magnified by great bull's-eye lenses to over four million candlepower. Though other lights like those at Chatham, Nauset, and Provincetown were erected later and stand guard around the peninsula, this oldest one remains the strongest, shining twenty miles out to sea and bellowing its foghorn voice over fifteen miles of waves.

PROVINCETOWN FROM MACMILLAN WHARF

The heritage of Provincetown is clearly seen as a fisherman's nets frame the Heritage Museum of Provincetown. Because of the town's isolation, it is a "town born of the sea, rooted in soil made by the sea" to quote its Chamber of Commerce. The type of livelihood gained from the sea has been varied. As a whaling center, Provincetown was right on the heels (or should we say right behind the sails) of Nantucket and New Bedford, as her sturdy ships sailed into the Arctic after right whales and into the Pacific after sperm whales. Its fishermen also made regular trips to the Grand Banks, salting down their catches with homemade salt.

For over one hundred years the Portuguese strain has dominated among the fishermen, beginning about 1896 when over 2,000 Portuguese lived in the town. An annual reminder of their continuous presence is the colorful Feast of St. Peter and the Blessing of the Fleet which takes place the last Sunday of each June. This wharf, named for native son and Arctic explorer Commander Donald B. MacMillan, is the setting for the culmination of the fiesta weekend when the Bishop blesses each vessel as it passes in review. The ceremony is a reminder that Roman Catholics, who were late comers to the peninsula, now have the most congregations.

The heritage of Provincetown is more than fishing, however, and the town-owned Heritage Museum, which originally sheltered the Centre Methodist congregation, presents the many faces of this picturesque place. America's first art colony was born in this town under the leadership of the late Charles W. Hawthorne, and his former pupils now are the backbone of the Art Association. The Fine Arts Work Center, which began in 1968, is a winter community encouraging the arts with thirty-two Fellows, twenty-one in the Writing and eleven in Visual Arts. A resident staff includes ten professional artists and writers with a distinguished visiting staff. Theater too has been an integral part of the old town ever since George Cram Cook, his wife, playwright Susan Glaspell, and novelist Mary Heaton Vorse launched the Provincetown Players in 1915. Stars have shone here ever since, many in plays by Eugene O'Neill who wrote some of his works looking over the dunes to the sea.

62

VIEW FROM PILGRIM MONUMENT, PROVINCETOWN

Provincetown harbor was filled to the brim in 1907 when President Theodore Roosevelt arrived on the presidential yacht '*Mayflower*' to lay the cornerstone of this granite shaft, which is a memorial to the Pilgrims. President Roosevelt was accompanied by a thousand sailors and marines on seven battleships which shook the town with salutes. Individuals, societies, and governmental bodies contributed to the 255-foot monument, which celebrated the arrival of the Pilgrims November 21, 1620, and their month-long explorations along the shore before sailing to Plymouth. At the foot of the tall monument is a bas relief of the signing of the Mayflower Compact which took place in the harbor. The slender shaft, which is an eye-catching sight at night when flood-lighting makes it visible for miles, has a gradual ramp walk (alas, no elevator). The climber is rewarded by a spectacular view across Cape Cod to the Miles Standish Monument in Duxbury and even to Boston. The climb is made more entertaining by the commemorative markers from Mayflower societies and New England towns set into the walls.

64

TOWN SQUARE, CHATHAM

Chatham has been in the limelight ever since Squanto, Wampanoag friend of the Pilgrims, breathed his last here. Guide for the Pilgrims on a corn buying expedition, Squanto fell ill with fever according to Governor William Bradford in *Of Plimouth Plantation*. As he died, he requested his friends to pray for him and "bequeathed sundrie of his things to . . . his English friends, as remembrances of his love." Though no monument marks the exact spot of his death the site is reputed to be on the seaward side of Bridge Street.

A monument in town square does memorialize later Chathamites who acquitted themselves well. The square is close to Cross Street which once had the more descriptive name of Captain's Row. The latter is a reminder of the seafaring flavor of the town which gave innumerable captains to the Cape, including two who won the Congressional Medal of Honor for life saving deeds. (Anyone wishing to check the current flavor of the town's seafaring life should visit the observation deck of the Chatham Fish Pier where trapmen, scallopers, eelmen, and about thirty-five long-line vessels bring in close to five million pounds of fish a year.)

The First United Methodist Church, which overlooks the scrupulously landscaped town square, had its roots in 1799 when an itinerant preacher traveled down the dunes leaving small "classes" in his wake. The Chatham class became official in 1816 and built the first rough log meeting house in 1820. The third and present building was erected in 1849. Later additions to it include glorious Belgian and Tiffany stained-glass windows.

CHATHAM RAILROAD MUSEUM

The mournful whistle of a train sounded first in Sandwich in 1848. The line was pushed to Hyannis in 1854, reached Orleans in 1865, Wellfleet in 1869, and Provincetown in 1873. Poor Chatham had to wait until 1887 for a special spur. So perhaps it is fitting that this town has the one remaining railroad station that is all gussied up with a ticket office, clicking dispatcher's key, posted timetables, and enough memorabilia to make railroad buffs drool.

The Victorian-style depot on Depot Road saw action from 1887 to 1937. Over 22,000 passengers traveled the line each year. A repair shop, fuel tank, water tower, and a giant locomotive turntable were support systems of the puffing engines. In 1951 the abandoned station was given to the town and lovingly reconditioned for a museum. A red caboose from the New York Central line attracts visitors who can climb aboard and imagine they are on their way to Boston, as long as they pretend not to notice the tracks end 50 yards down the line.

Another railroad station worth a visit is at the Aptucxet Trading Post. Built under the auspices of President Grover Cleveland when the summer White House was at Gray Gables, the station was moved to the present site and opened for viewing in 1977.

WYCHMERE HARBOR, HARWICHPORT

This almost perfect circle of water was once a race track. A sea captain who retired after the Civil War bought a fast mare and created a half mile race track around a pond. As a break from working his cranberry bogs, he raced with other old timers for prizes like fifty bushels of oats. A hotel called Sea View stood on the north side and its wide veranda made a perfect grandstand. Many retired captains who could no longer race at sea, enjoyed carrying on the tradition with their horses on land.

The southern part of the track was very close to the shore and after several severe storms, the sea water broke through. The town fathers repaired the break twice, then decided it was better to have a harbor for small boats there and move the race track. So a channel was cut, the little pond dredged and soon boats of all sizes and types lined its shores. The name Wychmere comes from a cottage colony established in Harwich in the 1880's.

THE WATERWAY OF BASS RIVER

The Vikings were the first Europeans to cautiously navigate this waterway which would bisect the Cape if it didn't run into a dead end in Follins Pond. Chisel driven mooring holes at the pond's edge are pointed to by some as evidence that Leif Ericson wintered here in the year AD 1003. Though the Viking travels are obscured in the mists of history, there is absolutely no doubt that the river, which forms the southern boundary between Dennis and Yarmouth is a popular playground today. Sail and power boats cruise the river, while many head out into Nantucket Sound.

Nursery to seamen for generations, this land is still living up to her past reputation. The Massachusetts Maritime Academy at the Cape's neck is a college turning out officers for the Merchant Marine, Naval Reserve, Coast Guard, and sometimes even luxury liners. But the amateur too is in his glory here, whether out for an afternoon on the family sailboat or motoring out to sea for a day of fishing. The Power Squadron courses in boating safety and the Coast Guard auxiliary patrols are constantly coaching the neophyte sailors so they won't end up on the Coast Guard's casualty list.

WINDMILL HOUSE, BASS RIVER

Not all the houses on Cape Cod are saltboxes or the original Cape Cod style. There are many delightful modifications like this home overlooking the marshes along Nantucket Sound which was designed as a windmill house and built in the early 1950's. The privately-owned structure, not a working mill, is diminutive in appearance but spacious inside.

Seekers for the unusual can find other unique places of abode. There is the 1850 octagonal house on South Street in Hyannis owned by Captain Rodney Baxter, skipper of the '*American Belle*' and the '*Flying Scud*'. A more recent intriguing house can easily be missed. All that can be seen of Ecology House as one drives down Race Lane in Marstons Mills is a huge solar panel, but visitors who stop by in summer when the privately-owned home is open for inspection will find a house set into the ground. Steps lead to a sunken atrium. Rooms with glass walls are flooded with sunshine. It's a joy to see and the energy savings are immense. Farther west in Hatchville the New Alchemy Institute, Inc., is experimenting with windmills, solar equipment, and greenhouses that soon may be as familiar appendages to houses as television antennas.

HARVESTING CRANBERRIES IN YARMOUTH

From the air in winter dark red patches appear in surprising numbers creating a pleasing mosaic on the Cape landscape. Though these cranberry bogs have a different hue and character each season, they stand out particularly in the stark winter landscape, symbolizing how the cranberry industry pervades the Cape. Bringing sixty million dollars annually in growers' pockets, it is the major agricultural venture.

Henry Hall of Dennis is credited with pushing the berries into the limelight in 1816 when he noticed that sand drifting over wild cranberry vines growing in his wet pasture caused larger berries. He experimented a bit as did his watching neighbors. Soon cranberries were flowing off the Cape in record numbers and money was flowing back in. Captain Bill of Dennis expressed the current sentiment in *Cannonballs and Cranberries* by Fredrika Burrows,

> "There's nothing to me in foreign lands
> Like the stuff that grows in Cape Cod sands."

Harvest time in those days was a social event when schools were closed and everyone went to the bogs. Originally the berries were picked with long-toothed scoops that are now prized by antique lovers who sometimes use them as magazine racks or planters. Now picking is by machine and the boxes filled with early blacks, bugles, cherry, and bell cranberries are soon on their way to Ocean Spray Cranberries, Inc., the country's leading marketer.

76

THE KENNEDY COMPOUND, HYANNIS PORT

For slightly more than 1,000 days, this projection in Hyannis Port was a power center in the world. A traveler encircling the globe in 1974 found that a villager in remote India and a peasant in the Philippines nodded in recognition when they heard their new acquaintance was from Hyannis Port.

The late Ambassador Joseph P. Kennedy purchased the home behind the flagpole in 1926 for a summer residence for his family which included nine children. Though Joseph Jr., the eldest son, died in a plane crash during World War II, the other sons John, Robert, and the surviving Edward made notable careers in politics. To the left of the flagpole is the home of the late Attorney General Robert Kennedy. President John F. Kennedy received word of his election on November 22, 1963, in his home directly behind his father's in this picture. Edward Kennedy, who is a distinguished and influential United State Senator, has a home on nearby Squaw Island.

When word of the election of President Kennedy was flashed to the world, people descended on Hyannis Port to see his home which is on Irving Street. The Kennedys found crowds looking into their dining room windows as they ate and soon the stockade fence that now surrounds the Compound was raised. Though the Camelot years of the Kennedy era have faded, the mystique continues. A favorite tourist excursion is to the Kennedy Compound (best viewed from one of the harbor cruise boats) and to the Kennedy Memorial on Ocean Street. Here the town has created a curved stone tribute, adorned with the presidential picture and seal and by a pool. The memorial overlooks the sea that the young president loved so well.

OLD HARBOR CANDLE DIPPING, HYANNIS PORT

Along with cranberries and beach plum jelly, candles have been long associated with Cape Cod.

It began when First Comers sought a waxy substance to make candles since tallow from domestic animals was nonexistent. (The first cattle arrived in 1624 but it was a long time before tallow was plentiful.) The waxy berries of the bayberry bush which grew profusely among the pines seemed ideal. Experiments showed that candles made from their wax didn't melt or bend in warm weather, weren't greasy, and sent a pleasing fragrance through the house when extinguished. Since it took an enormous quantity, something like twelve to fifteen pounds of berries to make one pound of wax according to one authority, the help of children was enlisted each fall. Candles were made by boiling the berries, skimming off the wax, then laboriously hand-dipping the wicks innumerable times.

Nowadays modern methods have replaced old ways, though the process remains essentially the same. Visitors to the Old Harbor Candle Company in Hyannis Port and Colonial Candle Company in Hyannis can see candles being made and may choose from an assortment of colors, shapes, and fragrances that would have amazed our ancestors.

OLD INDIAN CHURCH, MASHPEE

The oldest church building on Cape Cod was built in 1684 on Briant's Neck. Richard Bourne, Sandwich missionary who had befriended the Wampanoags and assisted them in registering their ancient deeds to the Plantation of Mashpee, was instrumental in receiving a gift of lumber from a London benefactor. The hand-hewn lumber was shipped from England, hauled overland by ox cart, and was transformed into a simple one-room meetinghouse. In 1717 the church was moved to its present site near Route 28 and decaying timbers replaced. In 1923 it was renovated and in 1970 the little church was completely restored and rededicated. Summer visitors stepping across the huge millstone doorstep find a plain but pleasing interior, a reminder that sometimes there is splendor in simplicity.

Set well back from the sometimes noisy highway, the church is surrounded by gravestones, some very ancient. Headstones with Indian names like Chief Big Elk and Deacon Zacheus Popmonet testify to members who had responsibility for the parish in the past. Other outstanding leaders were Rev. Joseph Amos and Rev. Simon Popmonet who succeeded Bourne as pastor. Popmonet was the first native minister in New England and served his flock for over forty years. Amos, blind clergyman ordained in 1830, had a marvelous memory and a distinguished ministry. Newer headstones proclaim quietly that there is still a congregation here, though the old church is reserved for special events, with regular services and most activities taking place in the Mashpee Baptist Church.

AQUA CATS OFF FALMOUTH

Any summer Sunday watchers from almost any beach can spot bright sails moving in concert as if directed by an unseen baton. It is merely a sailing race. Cape Codders are mad about them. Though these boats happen to be competing in Falmouth, the scene could be anywhere. As Joan Bentinck-Smith says in the maritime chapter of *The Seven Villages of Barnstable,* "Sails of every size dot the bays. Some of the classes are Prams, Wianno Seniors and Juniors, Lasers, Enterprise, Rhodes 18, Daysailers, Beetles, Sailfish, and other board boats: Knockabouts, Cotuit Skiffs, and Hobie Cats."

Sailors start young. The Cotuit Mosquito Yacht Club of 1906 was one of the first Junior Clubs in America. No male chauvinism here, for girls voted and held office. Even today no one over twenty-five in the organization can vote. Sailing is embraced by all ages. Yacht clubs preside over every bay and the title "Commodore" is an honor. President John F. Kennedy found relaxation sailing off Hyannis Port in the *Victura,* a Wianno Senior, and in the *Marlin.* He had fallen in love with sailing as a youth when he raced in Cape waters first in the Star class and later in Seniors.

FALMOUTH PLAYHOUSE

One of the most beautiful "star houses" in the country is in a natural woodland setting overlooking Coonamessett Pond. Opened in 1949 by Richard Aldrich, international theater impressario, it was the culmination of a dream. Though the Cape Playhouse in Dennis was his first Cape venture, this newer one was designed to his own specifications and included facilities for every facet of the operation. A glassed-in dining area makes possible a total theater experience from dinner before the show to shopping in the specialty shops and parties afterwards in the night club. Even the stage, back stage, and offices are spacious, helping to replace the dilapidated straw-hat concept of summer theater with one of luxury and elegance. The galaxy of stars on that opening season in 1949 included Tallulah Bankhead, Cedric Hardwick, Sylvia Sidney, Joan Blondell, Helen Hayes, Sarah Churchill, and Gertrude Lawrence. Equally as many luminaries appear each summer to grace the stage and occupy Star Cottage.

Falmouth also has one of the prettiest village greens on the Cape. It is worth driving a bit farther to the town's center to see the stately homes that edge the green which is presided over by two churches. One of the most imposing houses, owned now by the Falmouth Historical Society, was originally the property of Dr. Francis Wicks who was instrumental in the development of smallpox vaccine. The Society also owns Conant House next door and the Katharine Lee Bates House just down the street. Miss Bates, a professor of English literature at Wellesley College, was author of the hymn, *America the Beautiful*.

86

NOBSKA LIGHT GUIDES SEAFARERS

Unlike the bathers in the foreground, Nobska Light braves all kinds of weather to guide seamen past treacherous shoals into Little Harbor and Great Harbor at Woods Hole. In daylight weather flags have for years alerted small craft to what is ahead on fickle nature's calendar. At night the light, which unlike most beacons does not revolve, displays a white eye to seamen in safe waters and a red one if they have strayed too close to dangerous shoals. When fog rolls in, the rasping foghorn gives three short groans every thirty seconds and a radio beacon transmits the letter G every three minutes.

Nobska Light has claims to fame other than its non-revolving status. It is the only Cape lighthouse with rocks at its base, and until recently it was the only Cape Cod light with a civilian keeper. Now it is operated by the Coast Guard. The beacon first shone in 1828. Evidently there was only a minimum of equipment. When Captain Edward Carpender, United States Inspector of Lighthouses, visited ten years later, he recommended that a boat be purchased for the keeper. Things were better in 1878 when the government built a new, tall lighthouse made of steel. Since on this fairly flat peninsula high points are a rarity, Keeper John Scraff's remark in 1925 that on a clear day he could see the chimneys of New Bedford made the newspaper. The view at water level is spectacular too on a summer day. Aside from shapely bathers, visitors can see a veritable parade of small boats and ships from this vantage point which overlooks one of the busiest sea traffic channels anywhere around.

WOODS HOLE STEAMSHIP AUTHORITY

Any summer day cars stream down the one artery from Falmouth center to Wools Hole past the Coast Guard Station to the ferry slips and sea voyage to Martha's Vineyard or Nantucket. These offshore islands are close neighbors to Cape Cod and the ponderous ferries, which carry cars as well as people and supplies, are their lifelines. The hectic warm weather schedule of the ferries becomes more leisurely on the off-season and Locust Street residents, able to more easily leave their driveways, breathe a sigh of relief.

Martha's Vineyard, called Capawack by the Wampanoags, is the closest neighbor, less than an hour's sail. The first view of West Chop Light is a prelude to the delights of the triangular shaped island. Tiny gingerbread cottages at Oak Bluffs are a reminder of Camp Meeting days when a horse-drawn railway took Methodists to Wesleyan Grove and Baptists to their religious gatherings at East Chop. The twisted strata of colors painted gloriously on the clay cliffs at Gay Head is Wampanoag territory and a spectacular sight. The stately homes in Edgartown, site of Thomas Mayhew's first white settlement, recall its history as a whaling center.

The sail to Nantucket, the "Far Away Isle" of the Wampanoags, is about two and one-half hours. The entrancing living museum begins at the ferry slips with the Brant Point Light, second oldest in the country, and includes the remarkable homes such as the three bricks built by whaler Joseph Starbuck. Known also for its Quaker heritage, the island is also called the "little gray lady" of the sea.

WOODS HOLE'S SCIENTIFIC COMPLEX

Clustered together in an old whaling port are three institutions that have made Woods Hole famous throughout the world as a center for ocean and marine research. There are more scientists per square foot here than artists in Provincetown though often the latter seem to get the most publicity.

The National Marine Fisheries Service, run by the government, is the oldest of these institutions, dating to 1871. The Service is the support and hope of commercial fishermen, for its staff has a tremendous program of research in oceanography, ecology, physiology, and fish behaviour. Its scientists work with international bodies and it is not unusual to see vessels flying the Russian flag tied up near the moorings of the *Albatross,* the Service's 187-foot vessel which accommodates twelve scientists, has a crew of twenty-two, and a range of 9,000 miles. The Service is also responsible for an aquarium where harbor seals cavort in an outside pool, calling attention to the fish tanks, dioramas, and collections that line inside walls.

The Marine Biological Laboratory dates to 1873 when Harvard's Louis Agassiz collected a few students and taught marine biology on nearby Penikese Island. The privately-funded laboratory now has a staff of 375 and teaches 140 students each year. Its ship, the *Dolphin,* transports classes on watery field trips.

The newest facility is the largest and best known. Founded in 1930, the Woods Hole Oceanographic Institution employs 600, has three laboratories, and sends six vessels cruising the oceans of the world. The tiniest member of the fleet is the deep-diving two-man submarine *Alvin,* which is often in the news because it can go where other vessels cannot—like the ocean depths off Spain to recover an H-bomb. *Atlantis II* takes longer trips. A recent 18-month voyage took it 80,000 miles. The vessel's return coincided with the Woods Hole spring festival. The town was jammed. Bands played, whistles blew, and there was dancing on the dock as the ship moored.

Coming or going up Main Street, watch for one of the world's tiniest drawbridges which is no respecter of persons. It halts traffic when a sailboat leaves the shelter of Eel Pond for the open sea. Also, cast an eye on the fortress-like candle house where spermaceti candles were made in whaling days. It can be recognized by the ship model protruding over the door.

TWO OF THE THREE CAPE COD CANAL BRIDGES

The dream of a channel between Scusset Creek and Manomet River was a very old and persistent one. When the Pilgrims traded with the Dutch of New Amsterdam at the Aptucxet Trading Post in 1627, they portaged small boats across the marsh and lowland in between and thought longingly of a connecting channel. Samuel Sewall of Boston rode over in 1676 to see "the place which some thought to make a passage from the south sea to the north." George Washington saw its advantages in 1776 and recommended a survey. In 1898 the *Barnstable Patriot* noted the seven canal proposals before the state legislature, commenting, "Meanwhile, despite all threats, the Cape hangs on to the mainland with the grim determination characteristic of its people."

When financier August Belmont finally severed the connection between 1909 and 1914, bridges had to be built. Traces of those first abutments remain. Now there are three bridges, authorized by the government by 1933 and supervised by the Army Corps of Engineers, which is responsible for the waterway. One bridge is at Sagamore, gateway to the heavily traveled Mid-Cape Highway (Route 6). At the southern end of the canal are the Bourne and railroad bridges, the former framing the latter in this Bourne sunset scene.

The railroad bridge, which took two years to build at a cost of $1,800,000 is exciting to watch when a train is crossing. The vertical lift bridge has a 544-foot horizontal span which is suspended 135 feet above the water. When a train approaches, tower cables lower it like an elevator to permit the crossing, then slowly lift the span again. In recent years only a few freight trains have crossed each week. With the escalating energy problem, governmental and private bodies are making noises about instituting passenger service again.

94

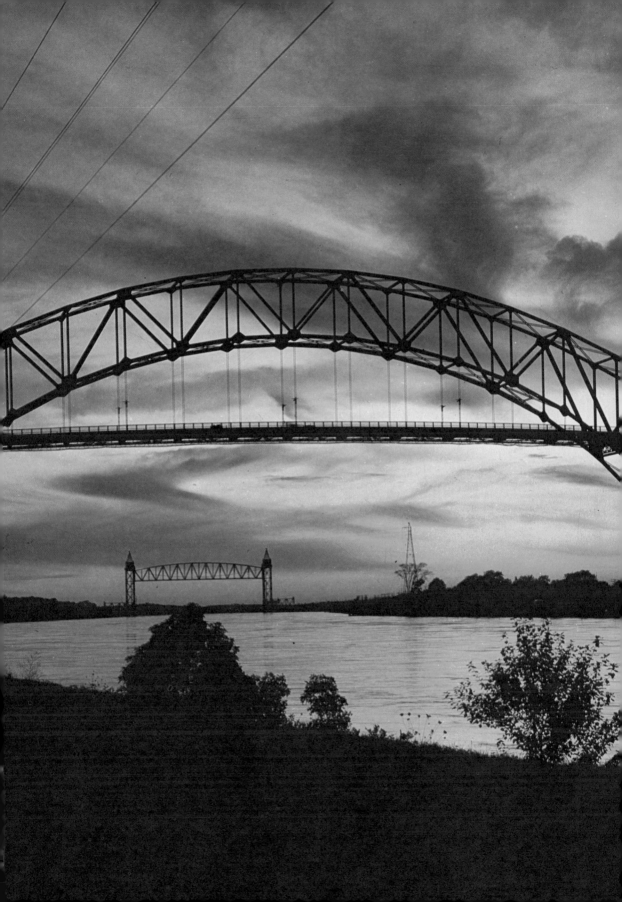